A Place to Call Home

*Following God's Design
for the Family*

Woodrow Kroll

BACK TO THE BIBLE
Publishing

A PLACE TO CALL HOME
Published by Back to the Bible Publishing
© 1999 by Woodrow Kroll

International Standard Book Number
0-8474-0696-2

Edited by Rachel Derowitsch
Art Direction by Kim Johnson
Cover Design by Robert Greuter and Associates

For information:
BACK TO THE BIBLE
Post Office Box 82808
Lincoln, NE 68501

1 2 3 4 5 6 7 8—04 03 02 01 00 99

Printed in the USA

CONTENTS

INTRODUCTION

Are you part of a family? Likely you are, but how do you define that family? What is a family anyway? Everybody thinks they know, but nobody seems to be able to put it into words. Perhaps a family falls into St. Augustine's timeless observation: "I know what it is until you ask me." The very fact that a family is hard to define is symptomatic of the problem.

Defining a Family

In the last three decades the legal system in the United States has hotly debated what constitutes a family. Some who are cohabitating but not married strongly advocate that the family should be defined as simply two or more people living together. It's little wonder; this has financial as well as social ramifications. In the United States, it appears that the tax codes often discriminate against the family. Frequently there are better tax benefits for two unmarried people who simply live together than for two people who are married.

The gay and lesbian lobby also wants the boundaries of the family redrawn. It has pushed hard to redefine the family as any two people living together regardless of their gender or sexual orientation. They want insurance and other social benefits that are usually reserved for heterosexual married couples. Homosexual men now adopt little boys and call themselves a "family." Lesbian couples also adopt "families." Ironic, isn't it, that it would be sinners in the midst of their sin who spark the heated debate on just what is a family.

Merriam-Webster's Collegiate Dictionary (tenth edition) defines *family* in a variety of ways. It says a family may be, among other things, all the people living in the same house; a group consisting of two parents and their children; a group of people related by blood or marriage; or all those descended from a common ancestor, tribe, clan or race. But what about those children who are adopted into a family? They do not have a common ancestor to their parents. They are not related by blood. But they are definitely part of their family.

The problem is that the word *family* is used in such diverse ways and there are so many variables that it is hard to clearly identify what we're talking about, let alone articulate how the family functions in society. Thus, many have come to use the expression "the traditional family" because of the numerous definitions for *family*. The traditional family consists of a father, a mother and their children. But even this is only traditional in some parts of the world. In many countries where *Back to the Bible* is heard, for example, a traditional family consists of a father, a mother, their children, perhaps their children's children and a grandparent or two. It seems that even traditionalists must be careful how they define a "traditional family."

Recognizing the cultural limitations of defining the family as a father, mother and children, we will still use that definition for the purpose of this book unless we specify otherwise. While extended families may be the norm for some parts of the world, the nuclear family—a husband, a wife and their children—is still the key to making a family function as God intended.

Setting the Boundaries

Edith Schaeffer, wife of the late Christian apologist and philosopher Francis Schaeffer, has proposed a unique analogy for the family. She describes a family as a versatile, living mobile made up of human personalities. Perhaps you've seen a mobile hanging above a baby's crib. It's there to provide entertainment. It spins in an ambiguous pattern at varying speeds. Each piece of the mobile appears to be doing its own thing, but actually it is inextricably linked to the whole by the strings that hold it in place.

Like a mobile, a family consists of a constantly moving collection of relatives blended together; people who laugh together, cry together, play together, live out memories together. The members change over time as some pass on and new ones arrive, but it is the family that gives form to this collection of related personalities. Like a mobile, within that form is the continual motion of each family member, independently moving, living his or her own life, yet remaining within the sphere of the family.

Because they are inseparably linked, each piece of the mobile affects every other piece. In the same way, each member of the family has an effect on every other member. Individuals in a family are constantly growing, developing, improving or declining. This happens intellectually, emotionally, spiritually and psychologically. This change affects the composition of the family, but as long as the related members are alive, they are family.

The Biblical Context

Throughout the Bible people have operated out of the family unit. On Passover night in Egypt, Moses instructed the elders of Israel to take a lamb for each family and kill it (Ex. 12:21). One lamb was slain as a sacrifice for one family.

When the law of the kinsman-redeemer was instituted in Israel, the instruction was that someone's brother, uncle, uncle's son "or anyone who is near of kin to him in his family" could redeem a person (Lev. 25:49).

Families even stood together in disgrace. Remember Achan? When he sinned by taking the spoils of war from the battle of Jericho, God identified Achan as the guilty party by having the Israelites line up by tribe, then by family and finally by household (Josh. 7:14).

The mobile that we call the family has always stood or fallen together. Families are like that. When functioning well, they are in constant movement, but they hang together. What is good for the family is usually good for the individual.

Damage Report

Unfortunately, vandals have entered the lives of some families and cut many of the strings. Parts of the mobile are now missing. Other parts are held together only by a frayed thread. Families have been weakened and some have been destroyed. The damage is severe, but the situation is not hopeless.

Some of these vandals include:

Adultery. Adultery has become the norm in the United States. Living with someone for an extended period of time either before marriage or in place of marriage is now a socially acceptable and widespread practice. One study indicated that situations of cohabitation have increased 443 percent since 1970.

But what is even more tragic is the number of spouses who are seeking sexual relationships outside of their marriages. Disagreement exists on the percentage of spouses who are unfaithful to their marriage partner, but in 1993 Tom W. Smith of the National Opinion Research Centers estimated that 15 percent of married men and women are committing adultery. Others argue that this number is not a true reflection of the situation because people tend not to admit their sin. A poll taken of its readers by *USA Today* in 1989 indicated 39 percent of men and 27 percent of women were unfaithful to their spouse.

Even if the lower figure is correct, this nevertheless translates into hundreds of thousands of families that are being weakened by infidelity. Since trust is the foundation on which a family builds a healthy home life, adultery is striking at the very basis of the family's existence.

Divorce. A couple of decades ago someone looked at the marriage and divorce numbers reported by the National Center for Health Statistics. The number of divorces for that year was precisely half the number of marriages. From that observation was born the myth that half of all marriages end in divorce. That is not true. When all marriages are factored in (not just the marriages that took place in one certain year), the divorce rate really is closer to 25 percent.

It is unfortunate, however, that among those recently married, the divorce rate *is* increasing. As long-term marriages move out of the statistical pool, chances are great that the number of divorces will inch closer and closer to that 50 percent level. That spells bad news for the family.

Study after study shows that divorce is a cancer on the family. Children from single-parent families are often financially less well off than their two-parent peers. They are also less likely to succeed in school and more likely to be in trouble with the law. In nearly every respect, divorce has a negative impact on the family.

Hope for the Family

But take heart. God is in the family repair business. He is able to strengthen the strings that remain and provide new ones to bind the family together.

Whatever state you find your family in, place your life and the lives of your loved ones into His hands. In God's Word you will find many promises to hold you steady. He has said, "I will never leave you" (Heb. 13:5); "I will guide you" (Ps. 32:8); and "My grace is sufficient for you" (2 Cor. 12:9). The testimony of God's Word is that "God shall supply all your need according to His riches in glory by Christ Jesus" (Phil. 4:19).

How can you claim these promises and make them real in your family life? How can you make your family a little bit of heaven on earth? How can you breathe a breath of fresh air into your family? How can you make sure your family is all God designed it to be? God's Word has the answers, and in the pages that follow we will explore what the family is by using analogies with which you are familiar. Use these chapters as a checklist for your family, and then pass this book on to others so they may use it in the same way for their family.

Remember, God loves families. He invented them, and He loves your family too. No matter what the quality of your family life is right now, you can look to Him to provide the means for improving it.

1

The Cornerstone of Society

*"No other structure can replace the family.
Without it, our children have no moral foundation."*
— *Charles Colson*

What is the most important stone in a building? The cornerstone, of course. A cornerstone is not simply decorative but is placed in a building for the benefit of every other stone. All stones are aligned with the cornerstone. If it is out of line, the whole building is out of alignment as well. As a result, the building will be seriously flawed and eventually may crumble.

Society has a cornerstone also—the family. God set it there. The family is His idea. It is one of only three institutions that was divinely established, the other two being human government and the church. It was God who said, "It is not good that man should be alone" (Gen. 2:18), and so He took Eve from Adam's side. Instant family! It is the most important unit in the world. It is the glue that holds society together.

If the family is out of alignment, so is society; when one crumbles, it's not long before the other does too. John D. Unwin, a British anthropologist, carefully studied 80 civilizations that have risen and fallen over a period of thousands of years. He discovered a similar pattern ran through each of them. In every situation the people started out with strong moral values and a healthy emphasis on the family. Over a period of time, however, the conservative attitudes became more and more liberal and moral values declined. Consequently, the family suffered. In each instance, as the family deteriorated, the civilization itself started to come apart. In all 80 cases the destruction of the nation was related to the destruction of the family. In most cases, that civilization fell within one generation of the destruction of the family unit. History proves that as goes the home, so goes the nation.

If society seems to be disintegrating before your eyes, it could well be because many families have already come apart at the seams.

The Threat to the Family

A threat to this cornerstone of society definitely exits. Throughout history there have been many serious attempts to destroy God's idea. In fact, you don't have to wait long after the first family was formed to see such a threat. When Adam and Eve had children, Cain and Abel, one of those children murdered the other and thus threatened the breakup of the family.

Wars, famines and natural disasters have endangered the family as well. Man's cruelty to man also has been a threat to this basic social unit. One of the most shattering aspects of slavery in pre-Civil War

America was the breakup of the family. Human beings were sold out of their families; mothers and fathers were sent to different places and the children put on sale like cattle. Whole families disintegrated at the auction block.

The Family Today

But at no time in history has there been a deeper danger to this cornerstone of society than now. The waning years of the 20th century were the most difficult ever on the family. And the basic threat is not slavery, not natural disaster, not even murder. The greatest single threat to the family has been premarital, extramarital and deviant sex. The gratification of illicit sexual desire literally has torn the foundation out from underneath our society and poses the most serious threat to God's institution of the family. A lack of self-control, godly morality and personal holiness, coupled with a prevailing desire for sensual gratification at any cost, have accomplished what nuclear bombs failed to do. Society is in trouble today because the cornerstone of society is in trouble.

Yet families have received another devastating blow—absent husbands and fathers. Too many families have lost their male role model. Men are simply walking away from their wives and abandoning their families in search of what television and movies lead them to believe is a more fulfilling lifestyle, a lifestyle unencumbered by family responsibility. Men have ceased being responsible men, men of God, husbands of one wife and fathers to their children. Instead, they have become playboys, seekers after their sexual fantasies. They long to live the lifestyle of the rich and famous but often have ended up reaping the consequences of the rash and foolish.

In addition, many families have lost the person who traditionally has been the center of the home—the wife and mother. Mothers have left the home in search of careers. They have learned that two incomes were needed to make the payments on the second car, the computer and the home entertainment system. Consequently, they have become part-time mothers and wives.

Of course, some mothers must legitimately work because of need. But many women have been duped into following the feminism frenzy that demeans the homemaker and ridicules motherhood as a valid career. Some women have fallen into the trap of believing that their self-worth is entirely tied to the business world and thus have eagerly entered what they disdainfully call the "man's world." These unhappy wives and mothers have left the home for a career not out of necessity, but out of a cause célèbre. They have championed the view that equality demands similarity and now many of them are living lives as empty as their male counterparts. Eternity will reveal that some leaders of today's feminist movement, both men and women, hold special responsibility for the disintegration of the family.

What women need are some champions like Sarah, Rachel, Mary and Naomi. These women were strong in character but found fulfillment in their roles as godly wives. There is still a need for homemakers, women who are the center of the home, women of skill and commitment, imagination and creativity. We need women who find their own needs met as they fulfill the needs of others in the family.

Living by the Book

These are not just old-fashioned ideas; they are God's ideas. Still, many modern families have abandoned God's Word as a resource for family living. Today many women get their information about the role of motherhood and the family from the parade of kooky characters who frequent television talk shows. Many men get their information about the role of the man in a marriage from the lascivious lifestyles they see on TV and movie screens or read about in magazines. Is it any wonder that families are in such a mess today?

The family is an entity created by God and protected by God. A Christian family is a unit of related people whose interests may differ, who may only slightly resemble each other, who have differing likes and dislikes, but who love each other and love God. They are people who want to build each other up. After all, God has an interest in the family's preservation. He instituted it as the cornerstone of society.

A Call to Action

When you see things happening that you know will destroy your family, don't take it lying down. When TV or other media depict situations that denigrate the family or show a family configuration that is unbiblical and unacceptable to God, don't be quiet about it. Write the program producer and voice your opinion. It's your right and your responsibility.

Take any and all steps to strengthen your family. If there are problems, get godly counsel from your pastor or trusted mentor.

Deny Satan the opportunity to destroy your family by denying him access to them. Vigilantly scrutinize what is coming into your home through TV, videos, magazines or the Internet. Get to know the friends your children are making outside the home and be aware of the activities in which they are involved. Don't let Satan camouflage his attacks on your family under the false guise of personal freedom. Be involved in strengthening your family.

The primary textbook on raising children, on marriage relationships and on strong families is your Bible. Don't neglect the Word. Do for your family what society cannot do: Give them daily doses of family medicine from the Scriptures. Marinate their minds in God's Word. Spend time together as a family and spend time in the Bible as a family. If you don't, you allow Satan's chisel to chip away at your precious family.

Commit your family daily to God in prayer and worship the Lord together in your church each week. You will not only strengthen your family but will preserve the cornerstone of society.

2

A Balanced Ecological Society

"A family is a unit composed not only of children, but of men, women, an occasional animal, and the common cold."
— *Ogden Nash*

In the last few decades much of the world has become environmentally conscious. We have taken to recycling, learning about the greenhouse effect and the ozone layer, mounting campaigns to save the whales and the spotted owl, and getting involved in just about every other politically correct cause that makes the news. And that's good. We are to be wise stewards of the resources and environment God has entrusted to us.

It's strange, however, that in an ecology-conscious world one ecosystem has continued to disintegrate: the family. Just from looking at the crumbling society around us, it's evident that the delicately balanced ecology of the family is being interrupted. And not enough is being done to save it.

Trouble on the Homefront

The reason the family is deteriorating is exactly the same reason the environment is having so much trouble. We have tampered with the ecosystem. We have allowed elements of God's delicate balance to be destroyed and that has resulted in the disintegration of the system in general.

Some years ago I read that Chinese farmers once killed millions of birds because these feathered creatures were eating their rice. They thought by killing the birds there would be a greater harvest. Instead, they discovered that yields went down. Why? Because the same birds that ate the rice also ate tiny insects. When the birds were no longer around to keep the insect population down, these tiny infesters did more damage to the rice crop than the birds did. These unwise farmers had upset God's delicate ecosystem.

When one tampers with the delicate balance in the natural realm, many people are up in arms immediately. Hollywood stars host events and loud cries echo through the halls of government for billions of dollars to correct the problem. Yet the most precious ecosystem of them all—the family—has been tampered with and very few even notice. In fact, some of the same people hosting events and appropriating billions for ecology have contributed greatly to the disruption of the sensitive equilibrium within the family.

God's Family Ecosystem

God built an ecologically balanced environment—the family—for the growth of human beings. Any family that operates within the environment created by God will be successful. But any family that abandons the ecology created by God is destined for failure. If this is true, it's important to become aware of what God's family ecosystem is like.

It was God's idea to place a man and woman together and begin a family. Time and again after each day of creation the Bible records, "And God saw that it was good" (Gen. 1:10, 12, 21, 25). But the first time God ever said something was not good was when He saw Adam alone in the Garden of Eden. "'It is not good that man should be alone'" (Gen. 2:18). So God created woman. Eve was not taken from Adam's foot to be trampled on or his head to rule over him, but from his side, to stand beside him as his equal. With that, God instituted this critical system we call the family.

It was God who told Adam and Eve that the next family would come about when man would leave his father and mother and cling to his wife instead (Gen. 2:24). This is the way God intended families to be perpetuated. One man. One woman. United in marriage for all time. Having children. These children in turn would grow into adulthood and leave home, and one man would join with one women to begin a new family all over again.

Sounds pretty old-fashioned, doesn't it? But it's God's balanced plan for the family. To ignore this divine balance is to tamper with a very delicate ecosystem. All you have to do is remove one of the elements, change the gender or role of one, and you throw the whole system into chaos. That's when families become dysfunctional and many are destroyed. When we tinker with God's plan, it's like shooting the birds to save the rice. The end result is we destroy not only the birds but the rice too. You just can't improve on God's ecosystem.

Family Diversity

Ecosystems are made up of diversity, yet it is a diversity that fits into a unified whole. That's the way the family is. God made great diversity between men and women. Most noticeable are the physiological differences. Men tend to be bigger than women, with larger frames and bodies. They are built for harder labor with greater upper-body strength. But the physical diversity is not the only diversity.

Emotional diversity is equally evident between men and women. Women are usually more sensitive and relational than men. We talk about "mothering" as a caring, nuzzling act for an infant. But we never talk about "fathering" that way. How men and women express their emotions is extremely different.

The interests of men and women tend to be divergent as well. Some of the stereotypical roles we have created for the different genders don't hold much water anymore. I was deeply embarrassed one day on an airplane by some rude businessmen sitting behind me when they learned that both our pilot and first officer were female. Their comments betrayed both ignorance and bad taste. Men and woman share most occupations today, but it's still true that many interests men have are not shared by women, and vice versa.

God made men and women different, and as the French are fond of saying, *Vive la différence.* But today these differences are being disturbed. The distinctions are being blurred. Unisex salons cut hair for both men and women, and sometimes it's the same cut. Clothing is being designed to further obscure the differences.

No thinking person would advocate holding on to the old bastions of male domination or enslave women to the kitchen. But God designed the family with clear differences among its members and with a definite pattern—a male father and a female mother with children, perhaps even some of both sexes. God's plan was for two parents, not just one. His plan called for an ecologically balanced family, a family balanced by His good sense.

When God put Adam and Eve together and told them to be fruitful and multiply, the family embarked on a great adventure. Of course, man and woman were different, but they were put together to discover those differences—not just in their physiques, but in their minds, their emotions and their wills. They were to delight in the differences, not deny them. The plan was for them to explore their differences, not destroy them. When you destroy a mother and her role in the home, you destroy the home because you upset the balance of ecology God has established. The same is true with a father.

Ecological Destruction

Today many people live in an ecologically impaired home. Perhaps you are one of them. Maybe you are a single parent. You do not have the benefit of God's ecology. Your husband has walked out on you or your wife has left you. You're trying to cope; you're trying to make it from day to day. Anything or anyone that willfully disrupts God's family ecology is guilty of the worst form of ecological sabotage.

But there are other forms of ecological sabotage going on as well. In the mother's womb for nine months, a tiny baby is formed in a delicate ecology. This, too, is an environment balanced by God. It's interesting that many of the same groups who fight to save the snail darter and other marine life from extinction also march for a woman's right to abort her fetus. Many of the people who claim to be ardent environmentalists and who are serious about their efforts to keep a balanced ecology in nature also have lobbied to disrupt the balance of God's ecology in the home. They are blind to their sin.

Many who seek alternatives to God's balanced system in the family wouldn't hear of an alternative to our natural ecology. This is the worst form of pharisaism. It betrays a lack of respect for God's most precious ecology—one man, one woman, a husband and a wife engaged in the roles of father and mother, raising children in submission to their leadership for the glory of God.

The Perfect Ecosystem

Families don't live in a perfect ecosystem. They haven't since Adam and Eve were driven from the Garden of Eden. Happily, however, even though our families do not live in an unblemished world now and there is no such thing as the perfect family, one day there will be. Someday we will find ourselves at home in heaven, in God's family, where the environment will be without flaw and the family will be together forever.

Jesus is the ultimate homemaker. He said, "I go to prepare a place for you . . . that where I am, there you may be also" (John 14:2–3). Jesus is making a home for God's family right now, and it will be the perfect ecological balance. But until then we must put every effort into making our families a foretaste of heaven. Recognize God's delicate ecology and refuse to destroy it or tamper with it. Recognize that it is God's ecology and we can't improve on it.

Often you will find that the ultimate goal of two separate entities is unity or oneness. This is true for the family. Families are meant to operate as a unit, with one ecologically balanced system, and this can only be the case as we maintain God's ecology of one man, one woman and a godly family.

If you care about your family and the family your children will one day be a part of, make sure that this balance is maintained in your life. And if you're in a situation where the ecology already has been disrupted, make sure your children have the beneficial influence of a local church. In addition, provide the godly influence of a daily time when you sit down together as a family to read and study God's Word and pray. Give your family the benefit of tender, loving care. Don't permit anything you do to upset the delicate ecological balance of God's family.

3

A Place to Belong

"Family is where all of us are we, and everyone else is they."
                                        — *Rudyard Kipling*

Frank Sinatra used to sing, "Everybody needs somebody." And that's certainly true. But not only does everybody need somebody, everybody also needs a place to belong. And if ever there was a place to belong, it should be the family. Sometimes our families thrill us, sometimes they embarrass us, but they're always our family. When all other relationships go sour on us, when all other groups turn us out, God intends for the family to provide a place for us to belong.

A Shelter in the Time of Storm

Life can get pretty stormy. But when you need a place to come in from the rain, you ought to be able to come to the family. When you are a failure in the world, families should be there to comfort you and love you. When the Prodigal Son had his fill of the so-called good life, when he was tired of living alone in the world, he came back to his family (Luke 15:11–32). He came back to the place he belonged. When Jacob finished 20 years on the run from his angry brother, Esau, he finally came back to Canaan, back home to his kith and kin (Gen. 31–35). The family is a place to belong.

Each of us has a variety of relationships. We have employment relationships (those with whom we work), we have church relationships (those with whom we worship and serve), we have friend relationships (those with whom we play), and we have family relationships (those with whom we have biological or legal ties). But of all these relationships, at the darkest times of our life it's the family relationship that is the strongest.

Spice to the Family Life

Often families are composed of a healthy but far-ranging diversity. God made each of us in His image, but we are still as unique as can be. Diverse or not, the family is the place to belong. People can be different and not fit into a political party. They can be different and not fit into a particular church congregation. But diversity doesn't stop you from belonging to a family. In fact, diversity adds some spice to the family life.

God gave my wife, Linda, and me four children—four very different human beings, three daughters and one son. Some of my children are computer literate; for some a computer may as well be a paperweight. Mine is not a musical family, but our tastes in music differ greatly. I can remember back when one of my teenagers was going through life with a laissez-faire attitude and her room reflected that. Another of my teens seemed to put her clothes away in alphabetical order or according to color or some other regimented system. They were just as different as they could be. Still they belonged, all of them, to the family. They made up the diversity of our family.

Although many people are made to feel that they don't fit in this group or that group, the family is a place where everybody should be accepted. Although every member belongs to the family, families are places where you shouldn't have to fit into a mold. The family is a place to belong even when you're different.

The Source of Positive Reinforcement

Families should be sources of positive reinforcement. Among family members there is the potential for great creativity. One of my jobs as a parent was to stimulate that creativity, not to stifle it. If one of my children took his or her first creative step and I threw a wet blanket on that creativity, the first step would become a full stop.

For example, one day my daughter Tina came home from her art class in high school. She had painted a picture of a house with a white picket fence outside. I'm no art critic, but for her first attempt, I thought she did rather well. In fact, I immediately found a place to hang that oil on our family room wall. She was displaying the kind of creativity that only she among my children appears to possess. And I wanted to encourage it.

Sometimes children express their creativity in ways that parents don't understand. When my son, Tim, was about three years old, I heard screams coming from his bedroom. His older sister, Tracy, came running out of the room yelling, "It's Tim! He's hurt! Come quick!" Linda and I both rushed into the bedroom to find Tim sprawled on the floor holding his ankle and crying. When I asked what had happened, Tim choked back the sobs long enough to explain that he had watched the birds flying outside his window so he thought he'd try it. He went to the top bunk bed and jumped off. Tim flapped his arms, but to no avail. He was airborne for milliseconds and then crashed.

If I had been Tim's employer and not his father, he couldn't have gotten away with that. I would have to have less sympathy for such a creative spirit. But you can try to fly in a family; they may laugh at you, but at least you know you won't get fired or demoted. The family is a place to try your wings, as long as you don't take that too literally!

An Opportunity to Develop Socially

Another great thing about belonging to a family is that you have a built-in laboratory for the development of human relationships. Brothers and sisters have to get along, or at least learn to peacefully coexist. Parents also need to get along or the family disintegrates. Families are great for developing the understanding that people are significant, important and worthwhile because God made us so. We are His children and that gives us value. Within a family, we have the opportunity to discover how to live with others who are different and yet who belong at the same time.

Have you ever sat down at the dinner table with your family and thought you were at the Friday night fights? Doesn't it seem like things spill over at the table—tempers, I mean, not food? At the dinner table you learn lessons about getting along with others who belong in your family. The Book of Proverbs tells us, "Better is a dinner of herbs where love is, than a fatted calf with hatred" (Prov. 15:17). Family members like different foods, pursue different interests and express different tastes, but at the dinner table each one belongs.

An Occasion to Celebrate

Mealtime is also a good time to celebrate just being a family. Often it's around the dinner table when all the horror stories come out about what happened that day. But you know what? That's also the time our funny bone is tickled the most. That's the time we hear all the humorous things that happened that day. Yes, mealtime can be a great time for families. Too bad we now have microwaves and so many families no longer sit down together at the table. This can only contribute to a further disintegration of the family.

Families are a place to laugh at yourself and others. The Bible says, "A merry heart does good, like medicine, but a broken spirit dries the bones" (Prov. 17:22). I find mealtime to be the perfect time to pull together the diversity of our days and allow each member the opportunity to demonstrate that they belong to the family. "Anxiety in the heart of man causes depression, but a good word makes it glad" (Prov. 12:25). Let the good words flow each evening in your family, because after a hard day at work or school or in the home, we need to know there is a place we belong. We need to celebrate being a family.

A Special Place

Remember, however, that the Christian family is a microcosm of God's family. As individuals, we have been wandering out in the world, away from God, lost in sin. We don't seem to have any direction, any purpose to life, no place to fit in and be accepted. But God has created a family, His family. And God calls each of us to come home to His family, because the family is a special place to belong. When we trust Jesus Christ as our Savior, God makes us a part of His family and our wandering days are over.

That's what makes the *Christian* family so special. We know the family is a place to belong to each other. However, the Christian family is not only a place to belong to each other, but also a place for each other to belong to God.

When I look at my family I am reminded that each of us is part of God's family, and for that I'm eternally grateful. Each member of my immediate family is saved; they have come to trust Jesus Christ as Savior, and that adds to our feeling of belonging as a family. We belong together here in time and in eternity. We are part of God's family. If that's true in your family as well, you are indeed blessed.

If your home is not a place where your family members feel like they belong, why not ask God to show you how you can change that? Pray that God will give every member of your family the sense of belonging that comes with a Christian home. Ask Him to save any members of your family who are yet in their sins and give them a feeling of belonging, both to your family and to His family. After all, the family is a place to belong.

4

An Equal-Opportunity Employer

"A family is a place where principles are hammered and honed on the anvil of everyday living."

—*Chuck Swindoll*

Strange, isn't it, that most people learn little or nothing about finances while growing up.

I knew a young man who was elected treasurer of his class in college. Later he came to me as his faculty advisor and confessed that he had never written a check before in his life. This class treasurer knew nothing about money! In all his years at home, he had never been given the opportunity to handle money, to know how to use it and, equally important, how not to use it. I suspect this man's story is multiplied many times over around the world.

Families are God's training ground for financial wisdom. Christian families are where God intends for us to learn from His Word about the use and abuse of money. A family is an equal-opportunity employer in that every member of the family should be given the opportunity to contribute to the family's finances as well as draw from them and, in the process, learn how to handle finances.

Start Early

In my family, our children always worked when they became the age to do so, whether it was bagging groceries, flipping burgers, mowing the lawn or baby-sitting. Each member of the family was encouraged to be a wage earner for the good of the family. When my children got some extra cash from working, my wife and I used that opportunity to teach them some important lessons about money.

At the Kroll household we did not give an allowance. You may think that's cruel and unusual punishment, but let me explain. I always believed that giving an allowance was teaching my children the wrong values. The allowance system, it seems to me, is just a junior version of the welfare system in our society. I never wanted my children to think I owed them an allowance. Instead, at our home, we always used the free enterprise system. Because they were members of the family, each of my four children had jobs to do every day. In addition to taking care of their own room (keeping clothes picked up, furniture dusted, etc.), each of my children was responsible for such chores as taking out the trash, setting the table for dinner, vacuuming and feeding the pets.

Why did they do these things? Because that was the price of living in our home. You contributed. You were expected to be a part of the family. You didn't expect to receive because you were part of the family; you were expected to contribute. However, beyond those basic jobs each one had to do, there were many other things around the house that Linda or I set a price on. This job would be worth a dollar; that job would be worth three dollars. If our children wanted more pocket money, all they had to do was earn more, and there was always a way to earn it. The more they felt they needed or wanted, the more they could earn, but it was never just given to them. The children never received just because they were a part of our family.

Remembering the Source

The family should be a place where children are taught about the source of money. The ability to earn is a gift from God. Deuteronomy 8:18 says, "'You shall remember the LORD your God, for it is He who gives you power to get wealth.'" I wanted my children to know that money is not evil; it is God's gift to us.

I also felt my children needed to learn how to express their gratitude to the One who enabled them to "get wealth." The way to express gratitude is by giving back to God from our money. Each time my children came home with some baby-sitting money or when they had a part-time job and got a paycheck, they learned early that part of that belonged to God. Off the top they would put away a portion of their money to return to God. I wanted my children to know that gratitude toward the source of their financial gain required action, not just a quick thank you.

Proverbs 3:9 says, "Honor the LORD with your possessions, and with the firstfruits of all your increase." I take that *all* to be literal. We are to honor the Lord with the first of the fruit from every gain we make. God gets off the top, not a portion of what's left over.

Respecting the Importance

Children also should learn about the importance of money in the family. Money is not to be squandered or thrown away. Money that is hard earned is also deemed of greater significance because you know that if you lose it, you have to work hard to earn some more.

Remember the woman in Jesus' parable of the lost coin? She didn't have much, but when she lost one of her ten coins, it was important enough for her to sweep the whole house immediately just to find it (Luke 15:8–10). I wanted my children to know that money that is hard earned is also hard to replace and they should not buy things frivolously, handle it carelessly or take chances with their money.

The family is a great place to show children that money isn't just handed to you; it is earned. Furthermore, once earned it is easily lost unless you have learned how to handle it wisely.

Restraining Greed

But there are other lessons children should learn in the family about money. They should learn about the heartache of greed. Parents have a unique opportunity to spot and correct the child who has all the makings of a miser.

The potentially greedy child may not be the one who always wants to earn more. That may be just the more ambitious child. The potentially greedy child also may not be the one who always wants to save more. That may be just the more prudent child. No, the potentially greedy child is the one who grudgingly gives to the Lord, grudgingly contributes to the family vacation fund or grudgingly takes his or her turn at buying the ice cream cones for the family. Proverbs 15:27 says, "He who is greedy for gain troubles his own house."

Greed in a child is distasteful, but greed in an adult is disastrous. Unfortunately, if greed in a child is not nipped in the bud, it blossoms in adulthood. "The desire of the slothful kills him, for his hands refuse to labor. He covets greedily all day long, but the righteous gives and does not spare" (Prov. 21:25–26). So debilitating is greed to the Savior's service that one of the character flaws that excludes a man from being an elder in the church is being greedy of money (1 Tim. 3:1–7).

When you make your family an equal-opportunity employer, you clip the wings of greed. And the time to do some clipping is when your children are young.

Family Budgeting

Nothing curbs the desire to spend like balancing the checkbook. Thus, one good way to teach your children the value of money is to have each of them, when old enough, take a turn at working with the family budget. Let them manage the family finances for a month. Have them sit down with that stack of monthly bills and a calculator. (You may want to look over their shoulder and check their work!) Budgeting is a good lesson for young economists to learn. One day they will be handling their own funds and will have to make critical choices about the use of their money.

Weddings and funerals are the two occasions where Americans use the least financial sense. When my oldest daughter was married, Linda and I sat down with Tracy and explained that we wanted her to have the finest wedding money could buy—*our* money could buy. That meant it probably wouldn't be the finest wedding she had ever seen. But we had taught her to be mature in making money decisions and now it was time for her to try her wings for real.

We told Tracy that we would give her a specific amount for her wedding. It would be a good amount, but not an extravagant amount. We put the suggested amount in Tracy's checking account and told her to use it any way she wanted for her wedding. She would have to choose how much she wanted to spend for a wedding dress and still have enough left over for all the other expenses. She had learned well the financial lessons in our family. She and her husband, John, had a beautiful wedding, tastefully done and all within her budget.

The Credit Trap

Children also benefit from the family being an equal-opportunity employer when they learn the potentially devastating effects of credit. When we live beyond our means and borrow money in order to do so, we invite catastrophe. The time to learn that lesson is when your finances are small and the potential for disaster is equally small. It also helps to be surrounded by loving family members who really care for you and are supportive of your decision not to abuse credit.

But there is another credit lesson that children need to learn while at home in the family. It's the lesson about the danger of being a surety for another person. On many occasions the Book of Proverbs addresses the folly of being one who co-signs a loan or guarantees a loan. Proverbs 6:1–2 says, "My son, if you become surety for your friend, if you have shaken hands in pledge for a stranger, you are snared by the words of your mouth; you are taken by the words of your mouth." Proverbs 11:15 reminds us, "He who is surety for a stranger will suffer for it, but one who hates being surety is secure." And Proverbs 17:18 warns, "A man devoid of understanding shakes hands in a pledge, and becomes surety for his friend."

Those are pretty strong warnings, but they still need to be heeded today. At some point many college students or those just joining the workforce will be asked by a friend or roommate to co-sign a note. Our children's family experience should teach them what God's Word advises. Teach these financial lessons at home so your children won't have to learn them the hard way when they're out on their own.

Family Economics

The family is an economic unit. Each member contributes; each member receives. But along the way, important lessons are learned about contributing and sharing. Learning about money is more than just being able to pick out the best bargain at the supermarket. The family is the place to teach children about God's gift of finances, God's expectations with regard to finances and God's rules for handling finances.

You love your children, and one of the ways to prove it is to use their early years as a time of instruction. Teach them that the family is an equal-opportunity employer, and you will have done a lifelong favor for them. Your family is important to you and to God. Get them off on the right foot financially.

5

Values Clarification Center

"Today's children are tyrants. They disobey their parents, gobble their food, and tyrannize their teachers."

— *Socrates (circa 400 B.C.)*

Wouldn't it be great if you and your children encountered only those values that match the values of heaven? Someday that will be true, but not now. Today, news anchors, politicians, writers, musicians and entertainers frequently influence our values. Frankly, however, some of these people espouse values that are belched straight out of the pit of hell. That's why we need a place to clarify those values. God has given us such a values clarification center; He gave us the family.

Running the Values Race

Passing on values is like being part of a relay race. Unlike a sprint, a relay race calls for a long-term commitment. Being a member of a family that seeks to instill and clarify values involves an extended, multigenerational process as well. The baton is passed from runner to runner, each generation being instilled with the values of the preceding one.

Until a relay is won, the runners in the race fall into various categories. There are those who have run and are now finished. Their part is done but they eagerly watch how their teammates are doing. There are those presently running, carrying the baton at the moment. They are either trying to maintain the lead or making up lost time. Then there are those awaiting the passing of the baton so they can carry on the race. So it is with the family.

Hebrews 12:1–2 expresses this image well: "Therefore we also, since we are surrounded by so great a cloud of witnesses, let us lay aside every weight, and the sin which so easily ensnares us, and let us run with endurance the race that is set before us, looking unto Jesus, the author and finisher of our faith, who for the joy that was set before Him endured the cross, despising the shame, and has sat down at the right hand of the throne of God."

You and I are running the race today. Others await their opportunity to run tomorrow. Still others have run before and are now watching from the gallery. The baton (values based on God's Word) is what connects all of us together.

The Need for a Clarification Center

Values historically have been handed down from those who have lived before us, much like the baton is passed from one runner to the next. Each generation not only teaches time-honored values but explains why they are important. Yet today so much of that has changed. Many teenagers now get their values from television, MTV, movies or magazines.

Another major source for the ethical training that forms our children's lives is their schoolteachers. How much of the lifestyle of your child's teacher do you know about? What kind of ethical framework has your child received from the school he or she attends? If your child is part of a school system in which evolution is taught as fact and God's creation is laughed at as a joke, you need your family to be a values clarification center.

But the lion's share of the values imbibed by most teenagers comes by osmosis, from hanging out with their friends. Without the support of their family, many teens are totally at the mercy of the value systems of their peers. If your teens are learning about sex and relationships from the magazines they read and from the street talk of their friends, you need your family to be a values clarification center.

The family is God's values clarification center. Some families, unfortunately, have values that are not honoring to God. But if you have a Christian family, one that is in church and worshiping the Lord regularly, one that reads God's Word daily, then you have a significant source for clarifying values.

What is necessary for your family to be a values clarification center? What must take place for you to be certain that your family's values are pleasing to God? Let's think about several things.

Continual Training

There must be constant training in godly values within the family. That requires reading God's Word daily. Psalm 1:1–2 says, "Blessed is the man who walks not in the counsel of the ungodly, nor stands in the path of sinners, nor sits in the seat of the scornful, but his delight is in the law of the LORD, and in His law he meditates day and night."

Daily instruction from the Bible is the key to establishing a solid base of values. If you neglect a family time in God's Word, you may as well invite Satan to teach your kids his values. He certainly will. That personal time of Bible study, meditation and prayer every day with your family is the chief foundation for your children's values system.

In our household, when we had children at home, that time came right after dinner each evening, every evening, without fail. Now, that's hard. Many things try to encroach on that time, but we must not let them. We didn't answer the phone during that time; we didn't even answer the door. That time is too important. It's where the Spirit of God not only teaches us as a family the Word of God but also the values that all who love God should espouse. Don't neglect this family time. Continual training in God's Word is the first step in values clarification.

Constant Checking

Constant checking is another important step you

must take. What are your children learning in school? What values are they picking up from their teachers, from the classroom, from friends after school? If you say, "Well, I assume they're picking up good things," you deserve the Naïve Person of the Year award. The only way you know is to monitor what they are learning, to check up on what they are hearing and believing.

Many teachers welcome parents into their classroom. Others see your visit as an unwelcome intrusion. Those are the ones you want to sit in on all the time. Those are the ones who may well be instilling a values system in your child that is diametrically opposed to your own.

Your family time together each day is a good opportunity to find out what values your children are picking up outside your home. You won't always appreciate what values your kids learn at school. And the values of friends have a great effect on your children as well. If you are suspicious of a friend, you need a family setting in which your suspicions can be confirmed or denied. The family devotional time can serve as a great place to check up on the values brought into the home.

Reestablish Your Responsibility

If you've been allowing your children's values to be formed by their friends, you've been making a colossal mistake. If you've never checked up on what kind of values system your child is receiving at school, you just may be shocked. We parents have a divinely instituted responsibility to make our family a place where God's values system is learned, where the values of godly ancestors are instilled, where the baton is passed on in the relay race of family life.

The family is God's values clarification center. All that is learned in the world, from the educational system, from the secular media and from friends needs to be tested against God's truth. The best place for a Christian to do that is within the context of a Christian family, your own personal values clarification center.

Pray that those who influence your children's values the most will be godly influences. It would be wonderful if the school system where your children are learning their values, the friends they have, the television programs they watch and the magazines they read all would contribute to a values system that honors God. But I'm sure you're not naïve enough to believe that they do. That's why we must make our families a values clarification center where all of us—parents, teens and children—filter our values through the Word of God.

When we are faithful in our meditation on God's Word, when we take time to make our homes a little bit of heaven here on earth, when we honor God with our minds as well as our hearts, then we will be able to sort out all the values that we bring into our homes and discard those that are debilitating to our

Christian life. This is one of the great privileges and responsibilities of the family. Don't be ashamed to make your family what God designed it to be: a values clarification center.

6

Educational Sounding Board

"Insanity is hereditary: You can get it from your children."
— *Sam Levenson*

There is a tall tale about a boy who was found at the age of 12 being raised by a wolf. The boy had a remarkably high IQ. In fact, he was a genius. In just three years he finished both elementary school and high school. Two years later he graduated from college with highest honors in nuclear physics. He was destined for an extremely brilliant future, but tragically he was killed one day trying to bite the tires of a speeding car.

This story is spurious, of course, but it does humorously illustrate that intelligence is always shaped, in part, by our environment. Since the family is our primary environment during our formative years, the Christian home should be the major educational sounding board.

I spent more than 20 years teaching at the college and university level, but one of my favorite books is *All I Ever Really Needed to Know I Learned in Kindergarten*. While university education is valuable, most of what we learn that's really important, we learn as children and primarily from our family.

A Family-Based Education

If it's true that the family is the source of what's really important to know, then it's vital that the family takes seriously its function as an educational sounding board. The family should be a place for young minds, and not-so-young minds, to bounce ideas around and to learn what has the ring of truth— God's truth—and what does not.

The family has a strong responsibility to educate the children who are a part of it. "Train up a child in the way he should go, and when he is old he will not depart from it" (Prov. 22:6). Of course, the family is not alone in being an educational sounding board, even in the things of God. The prophet Nehemiah publicly taught the people out of the Law—reading the Bible and then explaining the passage he had read (Neh. 8). The apostle Paul gave private instruction to all who came to him while under house arrest in Rome (Acts 28). But the family always has been the primary forum for education. In fact, the American public education system is only a little more than 100 years old. Until that time, education almost always took place in the home with the parents being the teachers.

Furthermore, the control of education always has been from the home, until the last few decades when control shifted to communities and school boards were elected. Since parents are exercising increasingly little control these days over the curriculum in our school systems, the education imparted by the family has become significantly more important now than it has been. It becomes the family's task to supply the important information and godly values not being taught by the public schools. Sometimes it's the family's duty to counterbalance what is being taught by the public schools.

A Well-Rounded Education: Intellectually

The family bears the responsibility of training the whole person: intellectually, spiritually and culturally. Every area of life must be bounced off the sounding board of the home.

My family was the educational sounding board for the intellectual development of my children and, to some extent, for Linda and me. We all learned together, and we continue to learn every day. At our family devotions each night we used a prayer guide, among other things, that helped us as a family to pray for the world. I wanted my children to have a global view of the need for men and women to hear of God's redeeming love. The particular guide we used listed countries, mission agencies working in those countries, some statistics about the countries and, most especially, some prayer needs.

One night I noticed that my daughters didn't know the geographical location of many of these countries. With the changing names of nations in Africa and now Eastern Europe, one could hardly blame them. But I thought, *What a tragedy to have such a small grasp of our world.* Geography is one of those subjects about which students know very little. My family was no different. So I decided to use our family devotions as a way to teach geography to my family, myself included. As a result, we had our devotions with a globe in the room and we learned world geography as a family.

It is a family responsibility to stimulate the intellectual growth of every member. Don't hesitate to supplement, or even modify, what your children are being taught by those who see themselves as professional educators.

A Well-Rounded Education: Culturally

Families grow culturally as well as intellectually. The family needs to be the educational sounding board for family culture as well.

How sadly deficient we Christians are in cultural development. How rarely we take in a symphony, the museum or the art gallery. Yet in Old Testament Israel, the family was responsible to see that the culture of Hebrew society was passed on to its members. The Bible talks about the skill of the artisans who constructed the tabernacle. "And Bezaleel and Aholiab, and every gifted artisan in whom the LORD has put wisdom and understanding, to know how to do all manner of work for the service of the sanctuary, shall do according to all that the LORD has commanded"

(Ex. 36:1). Men like Bezaleel and Aholiab were as revered in those days as Christopher Wren or Frank Lloyd Wright are in modern times.

And what about the singers and musicians who played for the glory of God? They, too, were heroes in ancient Israel. "And the Levites who were the singers, all those of Asaph and Heman and Jeduthun, with their sons and their brethren, stood at the east end of the altar, clothed in white linen, having cymbals, stringed instruments and harps, and with them one hundred and twenty priests sounding with trumpets" (2 Chron. 5:12). Ludwig van Beethoven or Johann Sebastian Bach have nothing over Asaph, Heman and Jeduthun. Every person in ancient Israel knew these musicians. Fathers instilled in their children an appreciation for the culture of Old Testament Israel. Fathers and mothers today must do the same for the sake of their children.

A Well-Rounded Education: Spiritually

The family as an educational sounding board, however, finds its greatest deficiency today in the area of spiritual education. Parents often delegate the responsibility of teaching their children about God to the Sunday school teacher, the small group leader, the youth pastor or the Christian school teacher. Many Christian parents have abdicated their responsibility as the primary spiritual teachers for their family. They have forgotten that the family is God's frontline educational center, not the church or the school.

The commandment of the Lord to Israel was, "'You shall love the LORD your God with all your heart, with all your soul, and with all your might. And these words which I command you today shall be in your heart; you shall teach them diligently to your children, and shall talk of them when you sit in your house, when you walk by the way, when you lie down, and when you rise up'" (Deut. 6:5–7).

This instruction was not given to the professional teacher. Teaching the Word is not to take place primarily in the school. This is a family responsibility. The commandment in Deuteronomy to teach these words to our children is obviously referring to parents, not teachers. It is also referring to our homes, not the classroom. "When we lie down and when we rise up" can hardly be interpreted as anywhere but our dwelling place. Spiritual education is a family responsibility.

How to Do It

Maybe you realize as a parent that God wants you to make your family an educational sounding board, a place where your children can bounce off new ideas and prove old concepts. But how will you make that happen? What are the key ingredients in making your home the center of a child's education? Notice some important instructions in this passage from Deuteronomy 6.

First, what we teach must come from the heart, not just the head. We are teaching values as well as truths.

Parents are to love the Lord with all their hearts. Only then are we fit to provide the kind of instruction that will shape and mold the hearts of our children. The words God spoke are to be in the parents' hearts before they are on their lips, teaching their children.

Furthermore, not only are we to teach our families the facts about the Word of God, but we are to talk about His truths as well. Teaching and talking imply two totally different functions. Teaching is didactic; it is the impartation of truth and knowledge. Talking is the family discussing what was taught and how these truths apply to our lives today. This can happen only as parents and children take time to talk. Perhaps if parents consistently talked to their kids about the values found in God's Word they would have to spend less time talking to them about vices such as drugs and alcohol.

When was the last time you had a spiritual discussion with your children? When was the last time your whole family batted around truths that you heard in church or that you discovered in your Bible reading? If it's been awhile, there's no time like the present to begin. Make your family an educational sounding board.

Creating Opportunities

These things sometimes don't just neatly fit into a conversation. There isn't a clearly packaged time of the day that on your daily planner you can label "Discuss theology with the kids." But don't worry about it. These verses don't imply a stiff and stilted discussion anyway. They tell us that the family is the place where through casual conversation we can come to understand spiritual and eternal truth.

As a university professor I learned that a good teacher creates opportunities to teach; he or she doesn't just stumble upon them. If you want your family to be an educational sounding board, you'll find the opportunities and the occasions to talk about the things of the Lord.

You may think, *My kids don't want to talk about those things.* Perhaps you *have* begun too late. Maybe your children's lack of spiritual thirst is evidence of a dry spiritual atmosphere in your house. But don't give up. Take it slowly. Begin with a time of simple Bible reading. Prepare some challenging and thought-provoking questions for your teenagers. Show them the Bible has the answers. Commit them to the Lord daily in prayer, in their presence. Pray with them as they leave for school. Show them your spiritual interest in them. Ask the Holy Spirit to create a thirst in them. Do the right thing, and God will respond in the right way.

An Eternal Education

Making your home an educational sounding board does not mean you are against formal education. Far from it. You want your children to have the best education possible and that means the best teachers possible. And whether you realize it or not, parents are the best possible teachers for their children. Perhaps you can't teach them everything they need to know, but you can teach them the eternal things. The educational system of the world should supplement your family education, not supplant it. Schools are no substitute for a family education.

Besides, the really important things in life, the things that have eternal value, are not just facts and figures. These important truths are not likely to be taught to your children apart from the family anyway. With less and less morality being modeled in our schools, with God being ridiculed in the classroom, and with more and more humanism and evolution at the center of the curriculum, your kids need the family to be the educational sounding board for all they learn on the outside, whether in school or from their friends.

God has designed the family to be the center of education, the place where all new ideas are bounced off the touchstone of truth, God's Word. If you want your family to have the best education, give them a family education. Make sure that your home is a place where the things of God are learned, discussed and believed. That's the kind of education that will last a lifetime—and an eternity.

7

A Shelter in the Time of Storm

"The most significant enemy of the American family? The breathless pace at which we live our lives."

— *James Dobson*

It's a tough world out there. There are viruses, broken bones and torn ligaments. There are critical people, difficult tests and hard questions. Drive-by shootings, ethnic hatred and senseless violence mark modern society. Somewhere in this tough world we need a shelter. We need a place that offers, at least to some degree, protection from these storms. God has designed such a place. He has given us the family, especially the Christian family, to provide shelter in the time of storm.

Home is a delightful concept. It's like family. And when you put the two together, you have a dynamite idea. Your own family living together in your own home. Regardless of what happens in the world, we always must know that our family offers a place of safety and protection.

A Place of Healing

Think about it. When you are sick, in pain or suffering from the storms of life, where do you want to be? You don't want to be out on the street. You certainly don't want to be at the office. You don't even want to be in the hospital. Where you want to be is at home, with your family, with people who will sympathize with you and comfort and care for you. If your family can't provide that kind of shelter, who will?

Remember the last time you had the flu? You felt sick and achy all over. You only wanted to be at home, in your own bed, under the covers with your family there to wait on you hand and foot. That's what family means. That's what families are for. No one likes to be sick alone. I don't often get sick, but when I do, I want to be home with my family.

Do you remember the story of Peter's mother-in-law? She was ill and Jesus came to see her. Instead of being quarantined away from her family, she was in the midst of her loved ones. She was in the shelter of her home in the time of storm. Matthew 8:14–15 says, "Now when Jesus had come into Peter's house, He saw his wife's mother lying sick with a fever. And He touched her hand, and the fever left her. Then she arose and served them." Jesus provided the healing, but while she was ill, Peter's mother-in-law sought shelter in her home with her family.

And what about Lazarus? Where was he when he was sick? The same place. At home with his family. John 11:1 says, "Now a certain man was sick, Lazarus of Bethany, the town of Mary and her sister Martha."

Lazarus sought shelter from the storm. He stayed home when he was ill.

God intended for families to provide comfort for each family member when they are sick. That's the way it should be. At home we find understanding, nursing, care and love. We don't expect the world to give that to us, but we do expect it from our family, because that's what a family is for.

A Place of Provision

But life has many other kinds of storms. The storm of sickness is just one. What about those storms that come into our lives when we are down and out? What do we do when we hit bottom, when we can't care for ourselves, when we are penniless and in deep distress? God has ordained the family to take care of other members of the family. If you have a family, thank God for those family members who will provide for you when you can't provide for yourself.

It happens to many folks. After being out on their own for a while, they find they do not have sufficient funds to maintain their lives, to keep body and soul together. Where should they turn? To whom should they go? When they have a deep need, when they lack clothing and shelter, where should they look?

The Bible says they should look to their own family. Remember that strong admonition of the apostle Paul recorded in 1 Timothy 5:8: "If anyone does not provide for his own, and especially for those of his household, he has denied the faith and is worse than an unbeliever." Those are harsh words, but they outline an important biblical command. Families are to care for one another. I am to care for the members of my family. If I don't, I am worse than an "infidel" (KJV).

I find it strange that Christian families sometimes are not as close-knit as unbelieving families, for that runs contrary to God's design that family members look out for one another. We are to provide for one another, whether that means financially, physically, emotionally or spiritually. God wants the family to be a place of security for its members in the time of storm.

What about your family? Do you provide for the needs of one another? Do you look out for one another? When one family member is doing poorly, do you provide a shelter for him or her? When no one else will care for those who are down and out, the family is God's instrument of provision.

A Place of Comfort

But there's more. God wants our families to be a shelter when we fail. He has designed families to be a place where there are no failures, a place where we can go and feel good about ourselves even after we have bombed out in the world. God wants our families to be a shelter in the time of storm even when the storm is failure.

Have you ever failed at something? Maybe it was a new business venture. The ads promised that for a minimal investment you could make a fortune, but all you made of yourself was a fool.

Perhaps you left home because you saw your mother and father as failures. You were certain that you could be more successful than they were. You were going to be a big success, but you ended up being a big failure.

Maybe it was simply the turn of events in your life that produced failure. In the story of Ruth in the Old Testament, Elimelech and Naomi from Bethlehem were driven by famine into Moab. When Ruth, a Moabitess, married Mahlon, one of the sons of Elimelech and Naomi, they embarked on a beautiful life together. But it was short-lived. Mahlon and his brother, Chilion, both died, as did their father, Elimelech, leaving three widows, Naomi, Ruth and Orpah. Naomi encouraged the girls to return to their families in Moab, but Ruth refused, choosing rather to remain with Naomi, who had truly become her family. Things hadn't gone well in life for Ruth, but she knew that Naomi's home was a shelter in the time of her storm. That's the way it should be with us as well.

Then there's the classic story of coming home again. It's the story of the Prodigal Son, who found out what a failure one can be in the world trying to make it on his own. He left home with his inheritance and likely intended never to return. But things did not go well for him. He squandered all his money, took an inadequate job and finally had to return home, back to his family.

If ever there was someone who was a failure in the world, it was the Prodigal Son. But the father, at least, made his family a shelter even for those who failed. Who can forget the grand greeting the father gave his son when he came in out of the storm? Jesus said, "When he was still a great way off, his father saw him and had compassion, and ran and fell on his neck, and kissed him" (Luke 15:20).

God desires that we make our families a place of comfort. A place where all the members of the family know that when the going gets tough, there is always a haven to come home to. A happy haven where they can find understanding and a no-questions-asked reception. If our families cannot be that shelter, then those family members who are out in the storm today are going to search for another haven.

A God-Ordained Shelter

God wants the family to keep its doors open and welcome back all those who are being tossed and buffeted by the storms of life. Quoting *Mayo Clinic Magazine*, well-known radio commentator Paul Harvey observed, "'For the patients who have an especially difficult time after surgery, if they eventually recover, it is because there is a family member who gives them a reason to be strong and a reason to go home.'"

Parents, what about your home? Have you given your loved ones a reason to come home? Do you have family members who are in need, struggling to make ends meet and could really use your financial help? Is your home a safe haven or an impregnable vault? Perhaps you have a family member who is living far from God. Does that son or daughter know that your home is a shelter for him or her? Does your teen, or even adult child, feel he or she can come home to the family and find shelter? Whether or not they come home may well depend on what kind of reception they think they would receive if they took that step.

Maybe you have a son or daughter who just needs a letter or a phone call today to let them know that the doors are open. Maybe you have a father and mother who need to know that if their advancing age or ill health means they can't make it on their own anymore, there is a place of shelter for them.

Some of your children may be having difficulty right now and you don't even know it. Some of them have been away at college or the university and have not done well. They may want to come home and even stay home, but they are concerned whether they'll find home a place of shelter or a place of shame. Make your home and family a shelter in the storm for every one of your loved ones. That's what God wants, regardless of the kind of storm your family members find themselves in.

When God made a family, He made a shelter. Let your family be a shelter for you in the storms of your life. If you have wandered far away from the life of your family, why not head back home today? Your family will always be your shelter. That's God's design for the family.

8

Passage to the Past, Gateway to the Future

"A happy family is but an earlier heaven."
— *Sir John Bowring*

I woke up one day a few years ago and realized that I am middle-aged. Actually, unless I plan to live to be 110, I'm a little past middle-aged. Frequently when I am at a radio rally and meeting friends and supporters of Back to the Bible, many will tell me they thought I would be older; I tell them I'm working on it. And sometimes I really feel it, too. But I'm enjoying being in the middle years of life. Why? Because I have family on both sides of me.

There is a generation of family members who are my senior, my parents and their generation. And there is a generation of family members who are my junior, my children and their offspring. At my age, I'm in a position to enjoy the full range of family challenges. I have the opportunity to experience to the fullest the privilege of being a passage to the past and a gateway to the future.

The Past

In the Book of Joshua, Joshua told one man from each of the twelve tribes of Israel to take a stone from the Jordan River and make an altar to the Lord. He did this so that when children asked what these stones meant, the fathers could link their children to the past with this memorial. That event is recorded in Joshua 4. "This may be a sign among you when your children ask in time to come, saying, 'What do these stones mean to you?' Then you shall answer them that the waters of the Jordan were cut off before the ark of the covenant of the LORD; when it crossed over the Jordan, the waters of the Jordan were cut off. And these stones shall be for a memorial to the children of Israel forever" (vv. 6–7).

We need links to the past like that. We dare not forget where God has brought us from, as individuals, as families and as the church. Several times in the Book of Proverbs Solomon repeats what he says in Proverbs 22:28, "Do not remove the ancient landmark which your fathers have set." These ancient landmarks were for the benefit of every generation. They served as perpetual reminders of God's faithfulness to past generations.

Family Links

What are your family's links with the past? Some have created links with home movies. Others have baby books that note when baby's first step was taken or first tooth was discovered. Family albums are great links with the past. The family tree in a family Bible can be a passage to the past. Tracing your roots gives some insight into your family history. You may have your own ingenious way of making a passage to the past for your family.

But what about making a spiritual link with the past in your family? After all, if your second birthday (the day you were born again eternally) is as important to you as your first birthday (the day you were born physically), you should leave memorials to your spiritual heritage for your family as well. By making a spiritual scrapbook or a spiritual family tree, you can provide a spiritual passage to the past. Give the details of your life and salvation. Note what events surrounded your coming to know the Lord. Share how you felt at the time. Record events in your walk with the Lord that are meaningful to you. Make note of those spiritual landmarks that must never be removed. In doing so you build a link to the past for your family that is also a spiritual heritage.

Family Traditions

Do you have some ancient landmarks in your family? Today we would probably call them traditions. Some of them may be spiritual in nature, others not. Are there some family traditions that you are preserving and passing on to your children? Usually traditions are just things someone started doing and you've done so long that you don't even know why, but you can give them a new purpose—they can be a link to your past.

For example, in our family we made it a tradition to collect Christmas ornaments from all over the world.

Most of these ornaments tell the story of the birth of the Savior. Every year at Christmas we would give each of our children another ornament, complete with the story behind it—where we got it, what it meant, why the ornament was unique. Some of them are from Germany, some from Switzerland or Austria, some from Israel and some simply from the local novelty story. But each year as our children were growing up they received a new ornament.

When our children were married and moved away from us, they took their ornaments with them. They had more than enough to decorate their house that first Christmas of their married life, and they took a bit of Mom and Dad with them as well. They took a passage to the past and made it a gateway to the future. They took a part of the family.

Two Necessities

If you're going to keep your ancient landmarks from moving, two things will be necessary. First, someone in your family will need to become the champion for keeping the passage to the past. Someone will need to take the responsibility of recording those events in your family life that become historically noteworthy. And second, you will have to build your memory makers into your budget. Family memories begin when families begin, but often those first years of married life you are too poor to think about building landmarks. Unfortunately, it's too late after the children have grown up and left home to build such landmarks. You have to begin even when you seemingly can't afford it. That will require some financial commitment, but the benefit is worth the cost.

The key verses in the Bible that help me to understand this concept of the family's role as the passage to the past are 2 Timothy 3:14–15. Here Paul counsels young Timothy to "continue in the things which you have learned and been assured of, knowing from whom you have learned them, and that from childhood you have known the Holy Scriptures." Timothy's mother, Eunice, and his grandmother, Lois, were faithful in building a passage to the past. Theirs was a family faith, an intergenerational faith (2 Tim. 1:5). I don't mean to imply that faith automatically transfers from generation to generation. Each person must believe for himself. But the family creates an environment in which faith can flourish.

If you haven't already, start today building some memorials to faith. Use them as a passage to the past. Set up some spiritual memorials. Begin a spiritual scrapbook or photo album that will link your family to its heritage. You may not be able to recreate the past, but what you are doing today will be the past tomorrow. Start today.

The Future

There is also a key verse in the Bible that helps me understand the concept of the family being a gateway to the future. It is Proverbs 22:6, which says, "Train up a child in the way he should go, and when he is old he will not depart from it." The verses in 2 Timothy look back; the verse in Proverbs looks forward. The family does both of these.

God designed the family to link us to generations that have gone before us. But He also designed the family to link us to generations yet to come. You and I have the opportunity to prepare the next generation for the future they will face. It's a daunting task, but not an impossible one. "'With God, all things are possible'" (Mark 10:27). Here are several things you can do to prepare those who will follow you and establish your family as a gateway to the future.

1. Pray for Your Family

Pray for your children, your grandchildren, your great-grandchildren. I believe Satan has convinced many Christians that prayer doesn't work and so there's no use in praying. But that's not what the Bible says. Jesus taught His disciples, "Ask, and it will be given to you; seek, and you will find; knock, and it will be opened to you. For everyone who asks receives, and he who seeks finds, and to him who knocks it will be opened" (Matt. 7:7–8). Again He told them, "Most assuredly, I say to you, whatever you ask the Father in My name He will give you. Until now you have asked nothing in My name. Ask, and you will receive, that your joy may be full" (John 16:23–24). The apostle James wrote, "You do not have because you do not ask" (James 4:2). Don't let the Devil defeat you in the arena of prayer. God wants you to pray for your family. Have faith in God.

What should you pray for? Begin with the most important thing. Pray that your children and grandchildren will come to know Jesus Christ as Savior at an early age. That was my prayer for each of my children and God was good to me; He answered that prayer. Now I am praying the same prayer for my grandchildren. There is no more important prayer in my life for them. The time of a child's faith in Christ is in the hands of God, but the prayer for that faith is in the hands of the parents and grandparents. Make it a matter of daily prayer.

Then, once your family has come to trust Christ as Savior, pray that they will walk with Him in holiness all the days of their lives. I continue to pray for my adult children. I do not pray that my son will be a great preacher or that my daughters will be greatly used of the Lord. I'd like that, of course; what Christian parent wouldn't? But I've learned that God will use my children as He pleases if they are clean before Him. So I pray that God will bind the evil one and keep him from my children. Remember what Job did. Job 1:5 says, "So it was, when the days of feasting had run their course, that Job would send and sanctify them, and he would rise early in the morning and offer burnt offerings according to the number of them all. For Job said, 'It may be that my sons have sinned and cursed God in their hearts.' Thus Job did regularly."

Godly parents never lose their interest in their children being godly. Jesus taught us to pray, "Do not lead us into temptation; but deliver us from the evil one" (Matt. 6:13). That's my prayer for my children now: that they will walk in holiness and serve the Lord faithfully. Praying for our children, whether young or old, is something we parents can do daily that will please God and agitate Satan.

2. Teach Your Family

But there's more you can do to make your family a gateway to the future: Teach your children right from wrong. Teach them to love God and honor Him. Teach them the words of Scripture as well as its principles. That's what Deuteronomy 6:6–7 says: "'And these words which I command you today shall be in your heart; you shall teach them diligently to your children.'" Notice that this verse says that we are to teach our children "diligently." I believe this implies that family responsibilities are serious responsibilities and are not to be taken lightly.

We already addressed this passage from Deuteronomy in chapter 6, where we discussed making the family an educational sounding board. It cannot be stressed too strongly, however, that parents need to use the home as a place of instruction for young minds. Children are very impressionable, and they trust their parents implicitly. God has built those qualities into children for a reason. Christian parents must discover that the reason is so we can instill Christian values in our young people by instructing them in God's Word.

There is no better time than in family devotions to instruct your children in God's Word. The ages of our four children span almost a decade. That meant we had a set of teenagers twice. It's not easy finding a time when the whole family can be together, but we were committed to that time and we locked it in immediately after dinner each evening. We never allowed anything to interrupt that family time. Choosing topics was always a challenge too. It's not easy finding common themes of interest to teens and younger ones, but it can be done. The key is the will to do it. Make teaching your children the things of God a high priority in your family, and you will find a time and a way to accomplish it.

3. Prepare Your Family

Third, prepare your family members for the challenges they will face by giving them a godly example to follow. I think back in my life to my godly grandparents. My grandfather and grandmother were wonderful people. He was an electrician and a deacon in the local church. Both of them greatly influenced me as a young boy. They were simple folks, but very godly. And my father and mother were the same. They made a significant impact on my future by the examples they set.

Now it's my turn. I must be a godly example to my children and those who follow them. I want them to look back on me with the same admiration and respect that I look back on those who have gone before me. Because my children are grown and gone from our home now, I find myself in an even more important role—that of grandpa. At this writing Linda and I have eight grandchildren. Many of them are old enough to understand what the Gospel is and several have asked Jesus to become their Savior. That does my heart good!

Young, impressionable grandchildren watch their grandparents. They are interested in how we walk before the Lord, how we relate to God and how God uses us. Some time ago my granddaughter Britney asked her mommy what "Papa" (referring to me) does. My daughter found it hard to explain to a six-year-old an international ministry like Back to the Bible. She told Britney that Papa teaches the Bible on radio and television. That didn't satisfy her. My daughter explained Papa heads a worldwide ministry with offices in ten other countries. She was unimpressed. Finally my daughter simply said, "Papa tells people about Jesus," and a broad, approving smile crossed that six-year-old face.

We ought to have visions for the future. We need to involve our children in plans for the future. We need to spend time with them in their choice of a college or university. We need to be a counselor to them. We need to be a friend to them so when they want to know if that certain someone is right for them, they will feel comfortable asking our opinion.

A Constant Challenge

When the family functions the way God means it to, it provides a passage to the past. The godly inheritance of those who have gone before us is passed down to future generations. And it also provides a gateway to the future. The family creates a solid starting place from which to face the future.

But nothing ever stays the same. Every day you and I are either building that passage to the past and that gateway to the future, or we are allowing them to fall into disrepair.

It takes time to build. It takes energy to build. It takes commitment to build. It takes none of these to allow things to fall apart. So, which is it for you? Your family needs you to be a builder.

CONCLUSION

The happy family is like an intricate mobile, inter-connected yet moving independently within a divinely determined plan. When that plan is skewed, disregarded or disobeyed, happiness is the first casualty and the family is the second.

We all want to be part of the ideal family. We want our families to be healthy and happy. But often that's not the case. What's a Christian to do?

Here are ten ways you can make your family what God and you want it to be, ten ways to repair some of the cracks that may have shown up in the cornerstone of society, to have the family that others only dream of.

1. Early on introduce your children to God's way of salvation and consistently pray for faith to take root in their tender hearts.

2. Nourish your children daily in God's Word and instill biblical values in them so they can face life's challenges with the strength of divine authority instead of the weakness of human uncertainty.

3. Let your home be a place for your children to discover God's special gifts to them and where they can exercise those gifts without fear of failure.

4. Give your children enough space to make mistakes, but set the parameters so their mistakes instruct them without destroying them.

5. Dad, love your wife in such a way that when your children seek to know the love of Christ, they will have a living example of that love.

6. Mom, respect your husband with the dignity and honor due one divinely charged to be leader of God's most precious and delicate institution—the family.

7. Give your children parents worthy of their honor and expect them to respect those worthy parents.

8. Instead of provoking your children's anger, promote their love. If you irritate your children, their anger will be the result of your bad behavior.

9. Teach your children by example that service to God is the secret of true fulfillment in this life and the source of true reward in the next.

10. Let your home exude the love of God, and let that love touch each member of the family equally, fully and genuinely. There is no greater gift you can give to your family.

Remember, families are made up of more than one person, so you don't hold all the pieces to the puzzle of how to have a happy family. Sometimes your greatest efforts are thwarted by a family member who destroys one of the pieces.

As a parent, however, you do hold most of the pieces. If your children are still young, apply these ten suggestions consistently. Apply them lovingly. Apply them expectantly. And if some of the cracks that are showing up regularly in the cornerstone of society show up in your family, apply any of the suggestions that you still can. God is in the family repair business. He can repair your family too.

The family was God's idea. It was a good one, and it still is. Your family is God's good idea. Let Him make the best of His idea.

New Resources

INTERACTING WITH GOD
by Gene Getz and Claude King

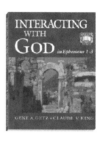

The best Bible study doesn't just give you information about God . . . it helps you achieve intimacy with Him. That's what you'll find in the *Interacting with God* series by Pastor Gene Getz and discipleship-training leader Claude King.

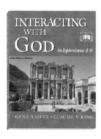

Interacting with God in Ephesians 1-3 and *Interacting with God in Ephesians 4-6* give you stories, outlines, word studies and questions designed to help you dig deeper into God's Word. You'll learn how to apply the Bible to your life through short assignments and personal reflection, and discover how to strengthen your worship experience through prayer exercises. So start interacting with God today!

Ephesians 1-3	0-8474-0200-2	$14.99
Ephesians 4-6	0-8474-0201-0	$14.99

A GIRL OF BEAUTY

by Carol Fiddler

In our culture of moral breakdown, character and values seem to be at risk of extinction. Author and mother Carol Fiddler urges parents to accept their

God-given authority and the high privilege they have to turn undesirable situations around by correcting their daughters' behavior and requiring accountability for the truth. Her new book, *A Girl of Beauty*, provides a needed tool for discussion, application and training in how to become a godly girl today—and a virtuous woman tomorrow.

Written especially for preteens, *A Girl of Beauty* addresses issues such as truthfulness, sincerity, service, respect and contentment. At a time when parents are crying out for answers and guidance in raising their children in a difficult world, *A Girl of Beauty* is a book they can confidently use to teach their daughters. *Available October 1999.*

Softcover	0-8474-1428-0	$10.99

VESSELS OF HONOR

by Woodrow Kroll

"Men of genius are admired; men of wealth are envied; men of power are feared; but only men of character are trusted." Becoming a vessel of service for the Master takes humility, loyalty and uncompromising obedience—all qualities Woodrow Kroll addresses in this new 366-page calendar with specially selected Scripture verses. Perfect gift item for a businessperson's desk, a mother's kitchen counter, a student's dorm room or as a present to yourself!

Available October 1999.

Flip Calendar 0-8474-1476-0 **$9.99**

Click and grow at
www.devotions.org

One of the best habits you can begin is to set aside time each day to study God's Word. You can easily accomplish that goal at our devotional web site www.devotions.org.

This exciting site features devotional thoughts from favorite authors including Woodrow Kroll, Elisabeth Elliot and Warren Wiersbe. You'll also discover classics from Back to the Bible's founder, Theodore Epp and meditations based on familiar hymns.

Bookmark this site, stay as long as you like and come back often. The more you do, the more you'll grow!